MW01246064

Standard Copyright Protected
1 Pound meals cookbook
By
Gary Bradshaw

Created and designed
by
Gary Bradshaw
www.garymbradshaw.wix.com/books

The food menus in this book are
used by myself, and all my friends.
A simple and easy way to stock up
for 3 weeks, and above all less time
consuming. I feel the days of adding
too many spices and ingredients to a
meal are a lot of my and your time
lost. Why not use one premade
product to take more time back into
your life.
I have, and I urge you to as well,
with my recipes.

Introduction

The main purpose of this cookbook is to be able to save you time in preparing and cooking your meals after a hard day at work.

When you come home from work, nobody wants to or has sufficient time to do the cooking. I will show you how to eliminate everyday sorting, preparing, chopping, mixing, and cooking.

These simple, easy to understand instructions are to cover a period of 3 weeks for 2 people.

Each menu has the quantity for the amount required, please review them carefully.

The idea is to prepare the full amount as shown on page 8, Dish out each portion for 2 persons into a container and then freeze them, once all 21 meals are prepared into containers, they then can be removed from the freezer before you go to work, and on your return the meal will be defrosted. Then pop it into a pan to heat & cook and add either Rice or Pasta, of which you choose for that night.

If you do not want to cover the said 3 week periods, simply adjust portions from ingredients list accordingly.

Introduction

Cooking does not have to be expensive or time consuming.

Through this book, I will show you how to Chop, Prepare, Cook, Freeze and Eat very Cheap, Healthy meals.

You will learn how to eliminate the extra fat, contained in most food before you cook it.

I will demonstrate how to peel an onion in 3 easy steps.

There will be no frying for periods of time or boiling water for hours.

These quick and easy steps will stock your freezer for 3 weeks.

So everytime you come home from work. No peeling, No chopping, No preparing, and importantly No stress.

Total ingredients for all meals

1 kilo	of	Breast of Chicken
800grms	of	Mince Meat
2 kilos	of	Onions
500grms	of	Mushrooms
1 Jar / Tin	of	Madras paste
1 Jar / Tin	of	Pasta sauce
1 packet	of	Maysan curry
1 packet	of	Pasta twists
1 packet	of	Rice
1 packet	of	York Ham
2 ripe		Whole Tomatoes
1 packet	of	Frozen Peas

Spices
Salt & Pepper

Information

All products are of Spanish bought and can be found in all countries worldwide.

Note
All ingredients are for specified amounts.
Pictures are showing ingredients only for a guide
Please read the ingredient list carefully before starting the process.
Half or quarter ingredients if you just want to cook 1 meal for 2 persons.

(This book is designed to allow you to prepare for up to 3 week periods using all the amounts shown on Page 8.)

Chicken Madras

Ingredients	Serves 8 persons
500grams	of Breast of Chicken
500grams	of Onions
250grams	of Mushrooms
Jar/ Tin	of Madras paste
Teaspoon	of Salt
Cup	of Water
Loose or Bag	of Long grain rice

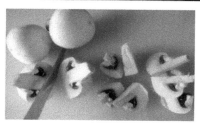

Pictures are showing ingredients for only 1 meal times 2 Persons.

To prepare & cook Chicken

Peel and chop Onions into cubes and place into a saucepan, add half teaspoon of salt. (You DO NOT have to put any oil or fat into the pan if you keep it on a LOW HEAT.)
Cook on a low heat until Onions are soft.
Slice and chop Chicken into cubes and add to onions, Stir in a tablespoon of Madras paste. Stir in ½ of a cup of water. Stir until Chicken is white, then add Mushrooms. Increase heat and add water as needed for preferred sauce thickness.
Bring to heat stirring occasionally.
Allow to cool and place evenly into 4 containers and Freeze. Each container serves 2 persons.

To serve
Cook rice to required preference.

Tips & Ideas on how to cook Rice, Pictures opposite, also at back of book.

Defrost Chicken Madras from Freezer, Reheat until hot and then add to rice

Hot Pasta Twists

Ingredients	Serves 4 persons
200grams	of Pasta Twists
400grams	of Mince meat
500grams	of Onions
250grams	of Mushrooms
Jar/ Tin	of Napolitano Pasta
Teaspoon	of Salt
Cup	of Water

To cook Pasta meat sauce

Peel and chop Onions into cubes and place into a Frying pan, add half teaspoon of Salt, Cook on a <u>low heat</u> until Onions are soft. Remove Onions from pan, Then add Mince meat, Cook Mince meat until brown, then drain away excess fat.

Return to frying pan Onions and Mince and then add Mushrooms and Napolitano Pasta sauce. Increase heat and add water as needed for preferred sauce thickness. Bring to boil and then Simmer for ten minutes. Cool and place into plastic containers and Freeze.

<u>To cook Pasta</u>

Boil saucepan of water, then add Pasta, simmer for 10 minutes. Then drain off the water.

<u>To serve</u>

Place Pasta back into saucepan and add in the <u>Defrosted</u> cooked Mince meat Napolitano Pasta sauce from the freezer. Heat until hot.

Chicken maysan curry

Ingredients   Serves 8 Persons

500grams	of Breast of Chicken
500grams	of Onions
A handful	of Frozen Garden peas
1in x 2in	of Maysan Curry paste
Teaspoon	of Salt
Cup	of Water

Loose or Bag of Long grain Rice

Rice ball in pictures is explained at back of book

Simple and easy steps to follow to make the perfect Chicken Maysan curry.

Peel and chop Onions into cubes and place into a saucepan, add half teaspoon of Salt, Cook on a <u>low heat</u> until Onions are soft.
Chop Chicken into cubes and add to the onions.
Stir in a 1in x 2in cube of Maysan Curry paste.
Stir in ½ of cup of Water.
Then add frozen Garden Peas.
Increase heat and add water as needed for preferred sauce thickness.
Bring to heat stirring occasionally.
Allow to cool and place evenly into 4 containers and Freeze. Each container serves 2 persons.

To serve

Cook Long Grain Rice to preferred taste.
Rice in a bag or loose rice in pan can be used.
See back of book for rice ball idea
Defrost Chicken Maysan curry from Freezer,
Reheat until hot and then add to rice

<u>How to peel an onion in 3 easy steps at back.</u>

Cold Pasta Twists

Ingredients	Serves 4 persons
200grams	of Pasta Twists.
500grams	of Spring Onions
2	Ripe whole Tomatoes
4 Slices	of York Ham
Teaspoon	of Salt

Perform the following simple easy steps, for an amazing cold pasta twist dish.

Chop Spring Onions into small pieces.
Slice and dice York Ham.
Slice and chop Tomatoes.
Boil saucepan of water, then add Pasta.
Cook Pasta until al-dente (firm but not hard) then drain and rinse with cold water to cool.
Place 2 pieces of kitchen paper towel into the bottom of the now cooled saucepan and tip in pasta, quickly remove the paper towel so as not to stick to the pasta, tap pasta dry when removing.
(As shown in picture 3 opposite.)
And then add in Onions, York Ham, and Tomatoes. Stir contents together.
Add Salt & Pepper to taste.

Eat straight away or Place contents into 4 containers & freeze

To serve
Defrost and Serve cold into a bowl.

Tips & Ideas

To cook Rice simple and easy

I brought a stainless steel Rice ball, you just place a handful of rice into the Rice ball and place into a deep saucepan, bring to boil and simmer for 10 minutes, the perforated holes helps cook the perfect rice everytime.

To peel an Onion in 3 easy steps.

Slice down at both ends of Onion (Do not go all the way through)

Slice across the Onion top to bottom & peel skin off. Hold down skin with knife and roll the Onion away from the blade

Chop Onions into cubes

All meals inside this book are for set cooked recipes.

<u>Alternatively</u>

Prepare and store all recipes
Raw and fresh (uncooked)

Preparing all the meals in one go may seem daunting, so what I do is allocate one evening, (I usually prefer a Sunday.) clear the kitchen of any unwanted plates, cups, trays, the sort of stuff that finds its place in the kitchen and never truly gets put into a cupboard. The reason I do this is so to make as much room as possible. I have found out over time, (to my annoyance.) that when preparing food in the kitchen you need as much room as one can achieve in such a small room. (For those who have big kitchens that part does not apply to you.) To prepare all Chicken meals you will need 16 small containers, 2 different chopping boards (or you can turn over the one you have or wash it thoroughly after chopping and slicing meat)

DO NOT CHOP VEGTABLES ON THE SAME
BOARD AS YOU CHOP FRESH MEAT ON.

<u>To prepare and freeze store cold, raw and fresh, all meals</u>

1 - To chop 2 Kilos of Onions is probably the hardest thing for many people. (My easy 3 steps on how to peel an Onion will help.) See p26. The 6x6x5 inch large plastic container.   (See p28, Pic 1.) is ideal to hold 2 kilos of Onions. So once the Onions have been Peeled & chopped, I place them all into the container and place a lid on top. (To protect your eyes from watering and to cover the aroma.)

2 - The 1 Kilo of Fresh Chicken, (UNCOOKED) can be sliced and cubed then placed in a similar large container 6x6x5 inch in size. (See p29. Pic 2.)

3 - Spread out 16 small containers onto, (I use empty butter dishes.) a large area. Place into each container a handful of Onions and a handful of Fresh chicken. See p29. Pic 3 / 4.

4 - Add in a Tablespoon of Curry paste, either Maysan curry paste or Madras paste. See p29. Pic 3 / 4.

5 - Stir together to marinate the Fresh Chicken, then seal with container lid. See p29. Pic 5.

6 - Place containers with meals inside into the freezer and take out accordingly. See p29. Pic 6

7 - For hot Pasta dish always cook mince meat first then allow to cool. Then add raw Onions and Napolitano sauce. Place 2 serving into 2 medium size containers & Freeze.

8 - For cold Pasta dishes chop Onion & Tomato & Ham, place into a container & freeze.

Pic 1

Pic 2

Pic 3

Pic 4

Pic 5

Pic 6

For more about Gary Bradshaw the Author.

Visit: sponsored links.

www.garymbradshaw.wix.com/books

Books Available from these sites

www.lulu.com
www.createspace.com
www.amazon.co.uk
www.barnes&noble.com
www.ingram.com
www.waterstones.co.uk

All food was brought at low cost supermarkets and some at discounted prices. Prices will and may be different in all supermarkets and retailers.

CPSIA information can be obtained
at www.ICGtesting.com
Printed in the USA
LVHW052309210520
656048LV00003B/374

9 781366 547378